Wealth Before 40

Proven Strategies to Build Financial Success and Live Regret-Free

Eric Graham

Copyright © 2024 Eric Graham

All Rights Reserved. No part of this publication may be scanned, uploaded, reproduced, stored in a retrieval system or transmitted in any form or by any means: electronic, mechanical, photocopy, recording, or otherwise without the express written permission of the author or publisher except in the case of brief quotations in a book review.

DEDICATION

I dedicate this book to my lovely wife in taking care of the house for me to work on this material.

ACKNOWLEDGEMENT

I am grateful to God Almighty for His leading by His Holy Spirit in helping me put this material together.

I am also grateful for all these individuals who have helped in making this project a reality:

Contents

DEDICATION 3

ACKNOWLEDGEMENT 5

Introduction 1

The Art of Making Wealth 9

The Art of Keeping Wealth 25

The Art of Multiplying Wealth 41

Build Your Wealth Through Investments 55

Live Below Your Means 69

Diversify Your Income Streams for Wealth Growth
.... 83

Master Debt Management for Wealth Preservation
.... 99

Conclusion 111

Introduction

Have you ever pondered the direction of your financial future? Right now, you could be asking whether you can achieve the financial independence you desire before turning forty or wondering how to accumulate wealth. Or maybe someone you know has already been on that route, and their hardships have shown you how important it is to act now, before the repercussions become unavoidable.

Many of us don't think much about our financial future as we go through our twenties and thirties. Trying to keep up with the demands of the present, paying our bills, and moving up the job ladder are all examples of how we frequently become enmeshed in the daily grind.

When you're young, this sounds like a sensible strategy, but the years fly by, and before you know it, you're approaching your fortieth birthday without a solid financial foundation. It's a sobering idea: what if you haven't amassed enough money to support yourself in your middle years, or worse, what if you have debt and other financial obligations that will cause you to suffer for many years to come?

The truth is that a lot of people don't have the money they need to live comfortably when they reach their forties. They battle growing debt, feel stuck in unappealing employment, or even have to deal with the unpleasant reality of an unplanned retirement.

Delays in financial decisions and a lack of strategic planning are frequently the causes of this. Indeed, according to polls, about 40% of Americans will have less than $10,000 saved for retirement by the time they are 40. This isn't the best situation for a happy and stress-free future.

However, consider another situation. What if you've already positioned yourself for financial success by the time you turn forty? What if you've amassed enough money to be able to spend your time anyway you like, knowing that you have enough to comfortably support yourself and your loved ones without having to worry about money?

The opportunities are limitless when you accumulate riches before the age of forty. You can concentrate on what really matters—following your passions, spending time with loved ones, and leading a free and fulfilled life—instead of worrying about expenses and making ends meet. Possessing financial stability can allow you to live life as you see fit, open doors to new opportunities, and bring peace of mind.

This book is more than just a list of theoretical guidelines. This useful wealth-building manual will teach you how to develop a strong financial foundation, preserve your wealth, and grow it in ways that will benefit you for the rest of your life. This book will give you practical strategies that you can start putting into practice immediately, regardless of whether you're just starting out, in your mid-twenties or thirties, or already feeling behind.

This book makes the straightforward promise that, by the time you complete reading it, you will have a clear plan for accumulating wealth before the age of forty, ensuring that your financial future is one of prosperity rather than survival. You will discover how to create, maintain, and multiply wealth, and most significantly, how to live a life free from the stress of unstable finances.

Here's what you can expect from each chapter:
Chapter 1: Learn How to Make Wealth

In this chapter, we'll explore the foundational steps for creating wealth from scratch. You'll learn how to harness the power of compound interest, the importance of starting early, and how to begin building multiple streams of income.

Chapter 2: Learn How to Keep Wealth

Now that you've started building wealth, it's time to preserve it. This chapter teaches the essential strategies for living below your means, budgeting wisely, and avoiding the pitfalls of lifestyle inflation. Keeping wealth is just as crucial as creating it.

Chapter 3: Learn How to Multiply Wealth

This chapter focuses on accelerating your wealth-building process. You'll learn how to leverage your skills and resources to multiply your wealth through strategic career moves, side hustles, and leveraging technology to automate and optimize your wealth growth.

Chapter 4: Build Your Wealth Through Investments

One of the most powerful tools for multiplying wealth is investing. In this chapter, you'll discover how to diversify your investments, minimize risks, and take full advantage of tax-advantaged accounts to maximize returns.

Chapter 5: Live Below Your Means: The Art of Financial Discipline

Wealth-building isn't just about earning more money; it's about controlling how you spend it. In this chapter, we'll explore the art of frugality, how to set clear financial goals, and the importance of financial discipline in ensuring long-term success.

Chapter 6: Diversify Your Income Streams for Wealth Growth

In this chapter, we dive deep into the importance of diversifying your income streams. Whether through real estate, dividend-paying stocks, or a side business, you'll learn how to create multiple sources of passive income that will help accelerate your wealth growth.

Chapter 7: Master Debt Management for Wealth Preservation

Debt can be a roadblock on your path to wealth. This chapter explores strategies for managing and eliminating high-interest debt quickly, leveraging good debt for wealth-building, and using credit wisely to enhance your financial opportunities.

There is no need for doubt or hopelessness on the path to financial independence. You don't need to question if you're acting appropriately or whether you'll ever catch up. This book offers the solutions you require, including tried-and-true methods that anybody can use to safeguard their financial future.

You can alter the trajectory of your financial future by putting the tactics in this book into practice. Realizing that you ought to have done things differently doesn't have to wait until you're forty or fifty. By the time you turn forty, you will not only be wealthy but also free to enjoy your life as you see fit, free from the constraints of money worries.

The time to take charge of your financial future has come. Are you prepared to live a regret-free life and accumulate wealth before the age of 40?

Chapter 1

The Art of Making Wealth

"The best time to plant a tree was 20 years ago. The second best time is now." — a Chinese proverb

Growing up in Pretoria, South Africa, Elon Musk showed an early propensity for entrepreneurship. He made the video game Blastar when he was twelve years old, and he sold it to a magazine for five hundred dollars. His enthusiasm for technology and business was stoked by this early achievement.

He attended a Canadian institution before transferring to the University of Pennsylvania, where he graduated with degrees in economics and physics. Musk thought that innovating in new industries will be the source of his future fortune.

Musk enrolled in Stanford University's Ph.D. program at the age of 24, but he left two days later to focus on his business endeavors. He co-founded Zip2, a business directory and map service for newspapers, in 1995 with his brother, Kimbal. Musk worked nonstop, taking showers at a local YMCA and sleeping in the office. Compaq paid $307 million for Zip2 by 1999, and Musk made $22 million from the transaction.

In 1999, Musk co-founded online payment startup X.com with $10 million of his earnings. Since online banking was still a relatively novel idea at the time, Musk encountered a lot of resistance. Nevertheless, he made significant investments to enhance the platform because he saw the promise of digital transactions. When X.com and Confinity, the company that created PayPal, merged a year later, the combined business concentrated entirely on online payments. Internal conflicts ultimately led to Musk's replacement as CEO.

Musk had a sizable ownership position in PayPal even after resigning as CEO. Musk took home $180 million when eBay paid $1.5 billion to acquire the business in 2002. He was already a multimillionaire at the age of thirty-one. Instead of focusing on his achievements, Musk placed his eyes on three sectors he felt were essential to the future of humanity: transportation, renewable energy, and space exploration.

In 2002, Musk used $100 million of his personal funds to launch SpaceX. The objective was to make life multiplanetary and lower the expense of space travel.

At first, the business had trouble, and Musk almost went bankrupt due to three unsuccessful rocket launches. However, SpaceX became the first privately funded business to fly a rocket into space in 2008 with the successful launch of Falcon 1. SpaceX's position in the aerospace sector was cemented that same year when NASA awarded it a $1.6 billion contract.

In 2004, Musk became a co-founder and investor in Tesla Motors, contributing $6.5 million to the electric vehicle start-up. Musk recognized the opportunity to use sustainable energy solutions to completely transform the automotive sector. He became CEO after actively participating in the company's business plan and product creation. By 2008, Tesla had introduced its first vehicle, the Roadster, which attracted notice for its cutting-edge performance and styling.

Musk had made a name for himself as a serial entrepreneur with several profitable businesses by his late 30s. In 2006, he co-founded SolarCity, a business that specializes in offering reasonably priced solar energy solutions. SolarCity swiftly rose to prominence as one of the biggest suppliers of solar energy in the US. Musk's fortune became even more diversified as his interests in technology and renewable energy grew.

For me, the life of Musk is one of those that demonstrates the art of wealth making. It doesn't only show how he made wealth, but also how he made it early I life, before 40. But one question that may be running through your mind is, what got Musk started in amassing wealth in the first place? The answer to your question is in the next subheading.

Work Is the First Step

The first stage in accumulating wealth is based on the most fundamental idea: effort. Without investing your time and energy in something worthwhile, you cannot build wealth. Your employment is the main source of income that will enable you to begin building wealth, regardless of whether you are working a regular job, managing a business, or pursuing a freelancing career.

The notion of having money without working is alluring, but in practice, building wealth requires dedication, perseverance, and a readiness to put your time and abilities into worthwhile endeavors.

Finding the perfect job that suits your skills and gives you a return on your time commitment is crucial. For some, this could entail landing a lucrative position in their area of specialization. For others, it could entail starting a business or pursuing a financially rewarding interest. Whatever the route, the fundamental idea is always the same: wealth starts when you have something worthwhile to contribute and are paid for it. The path to financial success is unattainable without this first phase of labor.

It's critical to understand that the nature of the labor is just as significant as the actual work. There are many methods to make money in the modern economy, and the conventional idea of working a 9–5 job might not always be the best choice.

While some people invest in highly sought-after, high-paying professions like technology, others achieve great success as entrepreneurs. Regardless of the path you choose, it is critical that the work you do has a significant impact on society because this will improve your capacity to provide a consistent flow of money.

Additionally, the concept of "work" encompasses more than only the cerebral or physical labor we perform. It encompasses the time and energy we devote to education, skill development, and maintaining our relevance in our respective fields. Consider those who work in technology. They constantly spend in learning new programming languages or tools that are in demand, so they don't just rely on their initial credentials to accumulate money. To guarantee that their companies expand and stay competitive, entrepreneurs must also make an investment in learning about their clients, rivals, and industry developments.

You may first have to work long hours and even give up personal time in order to create your revenue-generating endeavors. This is an essential component of accumulating money. Maintaining consistency and following the method is the difficult part. Many people give up on their goals too quickly, which prevents them from becoming financially successful. To get the money you want, you need to be patient and committed. You'll hone your tactics, boost your productivity, and expand your revenue-generating potential as you work.

Furthermore, changing one's perspective is necessary for accumulating wealth via labor. Instead of seeing work as a chore, you should see it as an opportunity. Your work takes on meaning when you accept that it will have a direct effect on your future financial stability.

This change frequently distinguishes the wealthy from those who are struggling financially. While others may see their employment as merely a means to a goal, the affluent see it as a stepping stone to higher things. This way of thinking has a big impact on how you approach your work, which eventually speeds up the process of earning wealth.

In the end, riches cannot exist without labor. It is impossible to ignore this fundamental step. It's about committing to a path where you continuously put in the work required to achieve the life you picture, not about looking for short cuts or methods to get around the effort that is required.

Create Passive Revenue Streams to Support Long-Term Development

True financial freedom is achieved by developing passive income streams that continue to produce cash flow long after the initial effort is made, even though active work is crucial in the early phases of wealth-building. Money produced with little active participation is known as passive income, and it is essential to ensuring that your wealth keeps increasing even when you are not working. You may lessen your dependency on active income and position yourself for long-term financial success by assembling a strong portfolio of passive income sources.

Making money through investing is one of the most popular ways to generate passive income. One common tactic is the rental income from real estate properties. After a property is bought and rented out, it produces a consistent income stream without needing ongoing maintenance.

In a similar vein, you can consistently receive a share of the company's profits by purchasing dividend-paying stocks. You can accumulate wealth with these passive income streams without having to put in a lot of effort to acquire every dollar.

Making digital goods or services that may be sold over time is another way to generate passive revenue. Writing an e-book, building software, or designing an online course are examples of this. With little further work, these things can be sold repeatedly once they are developed. The important thing here is that when you invest time or money initially, the product will constantly bring in money.

Scalability is a crucial consideration when creating passive income streams. Certain sources of income have a limited capacity to increase in value; for instance, a modest rental property may provide a steady income, but the amount of money you can make is restricted by the number of properties you own. Making scalable digital products, on the other hand, can increase your revenue without requiring you to put in as much work. Your wealth will increase more quickly the more you are able to utilize your time and effort.

However, there are risks associated with passive income. To reduce risk, it's critical to carefully manage your investments and make sure you're diversifying your sources of income. It can be risky to rely solely on one source of passive income in case it declines or becomes outdated. Even in unpredictable times, you can safeguard your wealth and keep increasing it by spreading your income among a variety of sources.

Furthermore, it is impossible to exaggerate the value of patience in generating passive income. Significant returns from passive income sources can take time to materialize, particularly if you're beginning with smaller assets. But over time, your wealth can grow enormously because to the compounding impact of passive income, which occurs when your earnings produce more earnings. Your money has more time to grow if you begin creating these revenue streams early.

Although creating passive income is not a quick fix, it will eventually result in a steady flow of cash that doesn't need ongoing work. while your money works for you even while you're not working, that's where real wealth is.

The Value of Making Wise Investment Decisions

Making thoughtful and strategic financial choices is essential to accumulating wealth over the long run. Your financial future depends on how you manage and increase your wealth through investments, even though working and generating passive income are also crucial. You may safeguard and increase your wealth with wise investments, guaranteeing that it will keep increasing in value over time.

Portfolio diversification is the first step to wise investment decisions. The process of distributing your investments over several asset types, such as stocks, bonds, real estate, commodities, and more, is known as diversification. By doing this, you lessen the chance that you will lose everything in the event that a specific market or asset class does poorly. For instance, your entire portfolio may be at risk if you only invest in technology stocks and the market declines. However, diversification shields you from the volatility of any one asset type.

Additionally, diversity enables you to benefit from market expansion. While certain investments might be more stable and yield consistent, moderate returns, others might be riskier yet yield bigger returns. You may make sure that your wealth increases consistently, even during uncertain times, by balancing your portfolio with both high-risk and low-risk investments.

Knowing the dangers associated with any investment is another essential component of wise investing. Risks associated with investments include the possibility of losing money or of passing up possibilities elsewhere. As a result, before making any financial decisions, careful study is crucial. This entails researching the market's stability, possible returns, and the state of the economy as a whole. Making better decisions can also be achieved by employing tried-and-true methods and speaking with financial consultants.

Dollar-cost averaging (DCA), which entails consistently investing a certain amount regardless of market conditions, is a well-liked investment approach. This tactic assists you in avoiding snap judgments based on changes in the market. You can lessen the effects of short-term market volatility and possibly raise your chances of obtaining a favorable long-term return by making regular investments over time.

It's crucial to frequently review your investments as your wealth increases to make sure they still support your financial objectives. As the market shifts, so too could your individual situation. Therefore, you may stay on track by periodically reviewing your portfolio and making any modifications.

Following trends without a clear goal or taking unwarranted risks are not aspects of smart investing. It all comes down to approaching the process of increasing your money with discipline, knowledge, and strategy. You can make sure that your money keeps increasing and standing the test of time by controlling risks, diversifying your portfolio, and choosing your investments wisely.

Thought Room

How might your long-term financial security be affected if you could begin investing only one year earlier?

How would you define "passive income," and which passive income source most interests you to pursue?

How can you strike a compromise between the necessity for long-term financial stability and the need for rapid returns on your investments?

Chapter 2

The Art of Keeping Wealth

"It's not your salary that makes you rich, it's your spending habits." – Charles A. Jaffe

The Buffet Story

Born in Omaha, Nebraska, in 1930, Warren Buffett's interest in money was evident from a young age. He made a little profit when he was six years old by purchasing six packs of Coca-Cola for 25 cents and selling each bottle for five cents. He had saved $5,000 from a variety of endeavors by the time he was a teenager, which is now close to $60,000. Buffett's propensity at reinvesting gains set the groundwork for his wealth-building ideology.

With $105,000 from friends and family, Buffett founded the Buffett Partnership in 1956 when he was just 25 years old. Using a value investing approach, he found cheap stocks with promising long-term prospects.

Buffett made sure his investments were supported by intrinsic value by closely examining businesses. In a few of years, his partnership was generating substantial profits, continuously surpassing the market and rapidly increasing his original investment.

Buffett's methodical approach to spending was one of his key wealth-maintenance tactics. Despite his increasing wealth, he led a conservative lifestyle, driving modest cars and living in the same house in Omaha that he had paid $31,500 for in 1958. Buffett supported reinvesting profits as opposed to treating oneself to luxury. His concept that real prosperity comes from building capital rather than spending it was reflected in his way of living.

Buffett's partnership had expanded to $7.2 million by 1962, with his personal stake amounting to more than $1 million. He concentrated on buying entire firms or sizable shares in enterprises that produced steady cash flow. He took over the faltering textile manufacturer Berkshire Hathaway in 1965. Buffett used the business as a vehicle for his investments, progressively turning it into a diversified holding company despite the textile activities' decline.

Buffett recognized the value of risk mitigation in protecting wealth. Famously, he stayed away from risky investments and took advantage of leveraged chances where he could reasonably predict the results. One of the best examples is his 1960s investment in American Express. Buffett made large investments and received big returns as the business recovered from a financial scandal because he saw the value in the company's strong brand and devoted clientele.

Patience was another key component of Buffett's approach. "The stock market is a mechanism for moving money from the impatient to the patient," he once stated. During market downturns, Buffett avoided panicking or following trends. Rather, he retained valuable assets, which made compounding advantageous to him. He increased his wealth to more than $25 million by 1969, when he was 39 years old.

Buffett was also an expert at using alliances and teamwork to increase riches. He established a network of trust and knowledge by associating with advisors and investors who shared his values. This strategy further shielded his money from needless losses by ensuring that his investments were constantly lucrative and well-managed.

Buffett's riches was maintained in large part due to his emphasis on long-term planning and financial knowledge. To keep himself updated, he read books, newspapers, and financial reports with great fervor.

Because of his unwavering quest for information, he was able to minimize errors and maximize profits by making well-informed decisions. By the time he was forty, Buffett had solidified his standing as a strict investor who not only created wealth but also protected it for future expansion.

Anyone can make wealth, but not everyone can maintain or keep it. It is a different ball game all together, which requires specific actions. Buffet has shown by his life that it is possible to keep the wealth you have amassed. He demonstrated that by his long term planning and continues learning.

Below are other actions that can help you maintain the wealth you have created for yourself.

Make Saving Your Top Priority and Live Below Your Means.

One fundamental idea is crucial to the idea of accumulating wealth before the age of forty: live within your means. The notion that wealth is reserved for those with high incomes is simple to fall victim to, but in reality, wealth is more about how you handle your income than it is about how much you make.

You're basically placing yourself on a financial treadmill if you constantly spend more than you make, and no matter how hard you work, you'll never get ahead. Living below your means becomes crucial in this situation. You may build the financial cushion necessary to save and invest, two essential elements of accumulating wealth, by spending less than you earn.

Being below your means is not always a sign of deprivation. It involves consciously choosing to put long-term financial stability ahead of immediate satisfaction. For example, you may decide to invest that money in a low-cost investment or a high-interest savings account rather than upgrading your vehicle or buying pointless technology.

The emphasis is on making better decisions that will eventually work to your advantage. You may make sure that long-term stability and growth, rather than ephemeral impulses, control your financial life by exercising discipline.

Simply setting money aside in a savings account with low interest rates is insufficient when you are able to save. Making saving a priority in your daily financial routine is the next stage. To ensure that you never miss an opportunity to save, you should automate as much of your savings as you can. This involves scheduling transfers to your investment or savings accounts on payday.

Saving at least 20% of your salary is a baseline that financial gurus frequently advise; if at all possible, strive for more, especially as your profession and income advance. The secret is to set up automated savings so you don't have to think about it.

Compounding is one of the most effective personal finance strategies, and it occurs when you put your resources into profitable ventures. Compounding is most effective when savings are regular and prudently invested. Your saved money eventually starts to work for you, producing more returns and quickening your journey to financial independence. The main tactic for accumulating substantial wealth before the age of forty is to start saving and investing early in life.

Living below your means has an impact on your emotional health as well. It eases the ongoing anxiety that frequently accompanies debt and unstable finances. You can guarantee your financial security and peace of mind by being proactive with your savings and putting your future above your present wants. This change in lifestyle makes your long-term objectives attainable by rewarding perseverance and self-control.

Steer Clear of Lifestyle Inflation

One of the biggest barriers to financial progress is lifestyle inflation, particularly as your salary rises over time. Many people make the error of changing their way of life to accommodate their increased income, which effectively results in their spending rising in line with their income.

Although this may seem like a reasonable reaction—more money should equate to greater comfort—the truth is that lifestyle inflation considerably slows down the growth of wealth. It's simple to believe that you should have a larger home, better clothes, or more lavish holidays when your salary rises. Every dollar you spend on improving your lifestyle, however, is a dollar that could be used to fund future expansion.

Keeping the same mindset that led you to begin building money is the key to avoiding lifestyle inflation. When your salary rises, utilize the additional money to speed up your investments and savings rather than expanding your lifestyle.

This may entail increasing your retirement fund contributions, buying assets that provide income, such as real estate, or diversifying your stock market holdings. Even if your income increases, you want to maintain a roughly constant level of expenditure. By doing this, more money becomes available for long-term wealth creation as opposed to being spent now.

Regardless of their income, many self-made millionaires are adept at being economical. They concentrate on making the most of their resources rather than giving in to the temptation to overindulge. For instance, people might decide to invest in real estate, which increases in value over time, rather than buying a fancy car. The basic idea here is that you have less money to invest in wealth-building vehicles the more you spend on material stuff.

The wealthiest people tend to have modest lives, according to research. Despite his enormous wealth, one of the richest persons in the world, Warren Buffett, still resides in the home he purchased in 1958. His method is not the only one. In order to focus on building wealth, many financially successful people consciously choose to live below their means and forego needless enhancements.

It's crucial to learn about delayed gratification in addition to avoiding lifestyle inflation. You make room for future prosperity when you resist the temptation to spend money on things that are not absolutely necessary. This entails establishing specific financial objectives and avoiding the temptation of transient indulgences that don't support your long-term financial security. Without having to worry about soaring costs, you can create a solid financial future with perseverance and discipline.

In the end, you can increase your wealth at an exponential rate by avoiding lifestyle inflation. You will have more money available for savings and investments if you practice financial restraint. By practicing this discipline, you can make sure that your growing money benefits you rather than hurts you.

Develop Your Budgeting Skills

Sound financial management is based on having a solid understanding of budgeting. A carefully considered budget gives you a concise, organized summary of your earnings and outlays, assisting you in making wise financial decisions. Making sure that your financial resources are going toward your priorities and goals is the goal of budgeting, not limiting your ability to enjoy life.

It's simple to lose sight of where your money is going when you don't have a budget. Small expenses that accumulate over time, such as regular dining out or daily coffee runs, are often disregarded. When added together, these ostensibly small expenditures can account for a sizeable amount of your income.

Finding these areas where spending may be cut with the aid of a budget allows you to free up funds for investments and savings. You may stay focused on long-term financial growth by setting a budget, which is effectively a financial plan.

The 50/30/20 rule is among the best budgeting techniques. According to this formula, you should set aside 50% of your income for necessities, 30% for wants, and 20% for debt repayment and savings. This rule's premise is to ensure that a sizeable amount of your income is allocated to wealth accumulation while maintaining a healthy balance between spending on lifestyle choices and requirements. Following this guideline or modifying it to suit your needs will guarantee that you're continuously saving money while controlling your daily spending.

A budget also makes it easier to monitor your progress toward your financial objectives. A budget enables you to understand how much you must save each month to reach your goals, such as building an emergency fund or saving for a down payment on a home. Your ability to forecast when you will reach your financial goals will improve with the accuracy of your budget.

Additionally, budgeting aids in debt avoidance. With high interest rates that make it hard to advance financially, credit card debt in particular can be a wealth killer. By ensuring that you stay within your means and resist the urge to overspend on credit, a budget holds you responsible. Long-term wealth building will result from increased opportunities for investing and saving brought about by this sense of financial discipline.

Finally, a budget enables you to plan ahead for unforeseen circumstances. Having a financial plan guarantees that you can manage unforeseen expenses, like medical bills or auto repairs, without letting them disrupt your efforts to accumulate money. You may preserve your financial security by setting up an emergency fund to pay for these costs after you have a budget in place.

You may take charge of your financial destiny by being proficient in budgeting. This straightforward but effective tool will help you make investing and saving a priority while making sure your financial objectives are continuously reached.

Thought Room

How well does your spending match your financial objectives, and where might you make savings?

If your income has increased, have you had to deal with lifestyle inflation? If yes, how did you handle it?

If you monitored every dollar you spent for a month, how would your financial condition change?

Chapter 3

The Art of Multiplying Wealth

"Wealth consists not in having great possessions, but in having few wants." – Epictetus

Boost Your Earning Potential by Developing Your Career

Increasing your earning potential greatly is the first step to accumulating wealth before the age of forty. Wealth creation frequently begins with a high income, but this calls for a calculated approach to professional advancement. Staying in your current role is insufficient in the competitive world of today.

You must actively look for methods to broaden your skill set, look for new chances, and take aggressive measures to position yourself for promotions, wage raises, and high-paying job offers if you want to genuinely boost your earning potential.

Learning and developing new abilities on a regular basis is one of the best methods to advance your profession and income. Developing skills that are in demand is essential to staying ahead of the curve in the ever-changing employment market.

Continuously expanding your knowledge makes you a more desirable asset to employers, whether you're learning a new programming language, honing your leadership and communication abilities, or obtaining credentials in your industry. Your chances of commanding more compensation and advancing into positions with greater responsibility and income increase with your level of ability.

Networking is a key component in raising your earning potential. Developing solid business links can lead to fresh opportunities that aren't always publicly announced. Through networking, you can access the "hidden job market," where a lot of high-paying positions are filled by word-of-mouth or referrals.

Make contacts with people who can assist you progress your profession by going to industry events and participating in pertinent internet communities. Additionally, this network can offer mentorship, which is a great way to advance your career.

Actively looking for higher-paying possibilities is crucial, in addition to networking and skill development. Many people anticipate increases to happen spontaneously after they land a comfortable job. However, you frequently need to take action in order to increase your pay. It could be important to look at chances outside of your current firm or even industry if you want to greatly boost your earning potential.

Strategic job switching can result in significant pay improvements, frequently far greater than what you would receive from yearly rises. Being receptive to new employment offers is crucial, particularly if they would enable you to advance in your career more quickly.

Additionally, don't be scared to haggle over your pay. Without haggling for a better offer, many professionals take initial offers or pay raises. You may significantly raise your pay by researching industry salary standards, recognizing the value you provide to your organization, and asking for what you deserve with confidence. Gaining the ability to speak up for yourself will eventually pay off.

Lastly, think about going after leadership positions in your sector. Although it takes time and perseverance to go up the corporate ladder, achieving higher managerial positions results in a significant pay rise.

Becoming a director, department head, or finally a C-suite executive are all examples of leadership roles that usually come with greater pay, bonuses, and other benefits. But advancing into leadership also necessitates honing your people management, emotional intelligence, and strategic thinking skills, so it's critical to cultivate these throughout your career.

Your income potential can be greatly increased by concentrating on career progress through skill acquisition, networking, strategic job changes, negotiation, and leadership development. You can attain financial independence before the age of forty by taking a proactive attitude to career success, which will lay a solid foundation for asset accumulation.

The Influence of Entrepreneurship and Side Projects

Relying only on your primary employment in the chase of riches may restrict your earning possibilities. This is where entrepreneurship and side projects are useful. You may build financial security and increase your wealth by spreading out your sources of income. Starting a side business or entrepreneurial endeavor that can augment your primary income or perhaps become your primary source of wealth is now simpler than ever thanks to the growth of the gig economy and digital platforms.

There are many other types of side jobs, such as consulting, launching an internet business, or freelancing in your field of expertise. The appeal of a side business is that it lets you capitalize on your current abilities and interests without requiring a substantial initial investment or high risk.

For instance, you can offer your skills to clients on freelancing marketplaces like Upwork or Fiverr if you have expertise in writing, graphic design, or digital marketing. These side jobs have the potential to be quite lucrative with the correct commitment and work, providing both short-term cash flow and long-term prospects.

Side projects are elevated to a new level by entrepreneurship. Starting a business can be a great method to increase your wealth if you have a passion or an idea that you think can address a need or solve an issue. Although entrepreneurship entails risk, it also has the potential to yield far greater returns. Entrepreneurship allows you to be in charge of your revenue, whether you're starting an online store, creating software, or providing a specialized service. Furthermore, having a business can result in a variety of revenue sources, including product sales, subscriptions, and licensing.

Scalability is one of the main advantages of entrepreneurship. A prosperous company can expand beyond what one individual can accomplish in a conventional position. You can create passive income streams and concentrate on expanding your company by recruiting staff or contracting out work. For example, you can scale and boost profitability without putting in more hours once your business is up and going by automating some procedures or assigning tasks to others.

Starting a business with little capital is now simpler than ever thanks to technology and internet platforms. For instance, social media is a potent and cost-free marketing tool that can assist you in expanding your customer base and increasing traffic to your goods and services. You can raise money for your company without the support of conventional investors or loans by using crowdfunding websites like Kickstarter or Indiegogo. With little initial investment, you may reach clients worldwide through online markets like Amazon, Etsy, and eBay.

Entrepreneurial endeavors and side projects can also offer worthwhile educational opportunities. Gaining knowledge about marketing, sales, customer service, business operations, and other areas will help you develop into a more well-rounded professional. The skills and information you acquire can improve your job chances and make you more appealing to employers who value entrepreneurial thinking, even if you don't eventually turn your side project into a full-time firm.

Starting your own business or pursuing side projects gives you access to more revenue streams, greater financial stability, and a quicker rate of wealth growth. Diversifying your income is a crucial tactic for reaching financial independence before the age of forty, whether that means starting a full-fledged business or making money off of your skills.

Use Automation and Technology to Increase Your Wealth

In the current digital era, automation and technology provide strong instruments for generating income. By utilizing these resources, people can increase their money quickly and effectively. You can raise your earning potential and accumulate wealth far more quickly than you might with traditional ways if you use technology to automate jobs, make better investments, and optimize other areas of your financial life.

Automating your investments and savings is one of the most significant ways that technology can assist you in accumulating wealth. You can set up periodic contributions to your investment accounts using automated investment options that are available from a number of financial institutions and investment platforms.

Without having to actively distribute cash, our "set it and forget it" approach guarantees that you constantly invest in the markets. Compound growth and this methodical technique can lead to substantial wealth accumulation over time. For instance, robo-advisors make it simple and low-effort for anyone to begin investing by using algorithms to manage and increase your accounts according to your goals and risk tolerance.

The use of online banking and budgeting applications is another way that technology can support wealth accumulation. You may better manage your finances and gain comprehensive insights into your spending patterns with the help of these tools.

By helping you make and follow a budget, apps like Mint and YNAB (You Need A Budget) make sure you live within your means and set aside money for investments and savings. Additionally, these apps frequently enable automated savings, which involves regularly transferring modest sums of money into investments or savings accounts.

Additionally, technology facilitates the expansion of your business endeavors. You may easily sell goods to clients worldwide with e-commerce platforms like Shopify and Etsy. You may set up automated systems for processing orders, taking payments, and even handling customer interactions with solutions like PayPal, Stripe, and Shopify Payments.

This enables you to avoid becoming mired down in daily activities and instead concentrate on expanding your business. In a similar vein, automation software can assist you in managing customer service, social media scheduling, email marketing, and other duties that don't require continual attention.

Technology has revolutionized wealth-building tactics in the financial world. By making it simpler for anyone to purchase and sell stocks, bonds, and cryptocurrencies, trading platforms such as Robinhood and E*TRADE have democratized investment. These platforms enable people to make educated judgments by providing real-time market data, instructional materials, and affordable costs. Additionally, by recommending varied assets based on past data and patterns, AI-driven investment systems can assist you in optimizing your portfolio.

Another way that technology supports wealth building is by utilizing digital technologies to leverage passive income strategies. For instance, you can make money from your material by setting up a blog, YouTube channel, or podcast and using affiliate marketing, sponsorships, or advertisements. Once established, these revenue streams can produce passive income for years to come, despite the initial time and effort commitment.

Numerous options exist to accumulate riches with little manual labor thanks to automation and technology. You may save time, cut expenses, and boost your earning potential by integrating these technologies into your financial strategy. This will eventually result in quicker wealth creation and financial independence.

Thought Room

Which talent could you learn today to boost your income potential in the upcoming year?

How may launching a business or adding a side gig help you generate wealth more quickly?

How can you keep on track with your wealth goals and streamline your financial management with automation tools?

Chapter 4

Build Your Wealth Through Investments

"Do not save what is left after spending, but spend what is left after saving." – Warren Buffett

Diversify Your Holdings to Reduce Risk

One of the most effective strategies for investors to control risk while pursuing riches is diversification. Spreading assets over a variety of asset classes, including stocks, bonds, real estate, commodities, and more, is a straightforward yet very successful strategy.

By doing this, you lower your chance of losing all of your money in the event that a specific asset class or market segment underperforms. Because various assets frequently react differently to economic conditions, diversification helps to reduce portfolio volatility.

The fact that various asset classes don't always move in the same direction at the same time is one of the primary reasons diversification is effective. Bonds and real estate investments, for instance, may be remaining steady or even rising in value during a downturn in the stock market.

On the other hand, bond prices may increase and stock prices may become more volatile when interest rates are low. The overall risk to your wealth can be decreased by possessing a variety of assets, as the positive performance of one can offset the negative performance of another.

It's crucial to remember that diversification should go beyond simply distributing investments among several asset types. Additionally, you should look for diversity within each asset class. You can diversify in the stock market, for instance, by owning a combination of small- and large-cap companies or by investing in several industries, such as consumer products, healthcare, and technology. Because real estate markets might act differently depending on where you live, you may invest in both residential and commercial real estate, or even assets in different geographical areas.

Being aware of the relationships between your investments is another aspect of diversification. Investing in a variety of assets lowers risk, but you should make sure that they are not all tied to each other. You are not genuinely diversifying your portfolio, for example, if you only invest in technology stocks, all of which are impacted by comparable market conditions. A truly diversified portfolio will lessen the likelihood that a single event or market downturn will have a detrimental effect on your finances.

Time horizon is another facet of diversification. You could wish to divide your capital between short-term and long-term investments, depending on your risk tolerance and financial objectives. While long-term assets like stocks or real estate offer greater potential returns over time, short-term investments like money market funds or short-term bonds offer greater stability and liquidity. A well-diversified portfolio takes into account both your wealth's long-term development potential and your current requirement for liquidity.

Periodically rebalancing your portfolio is also crucial. Your initial asset allocation may alter as a result of changes in the relative values of the various assets in your portfolio brought on by market fluctuations. Maintaining the proper mix of investments in line with your financial objectives and risk tolerance is ensured by rebalancing. Your portfolio may grow more strongly weighted toward one asset class without rebalancing, which could increase your risk without you being aware of it.

All things considered, diversification is essential to wealth management since it reduces risk and raises the possibility of consistent returns over time. To protect against market volatility, all investors, regardless of experience level, should include this method in their portfolio.

Recognize the Risk and Return of Your Investing

Risk and reward must always be balanced while investing. Knowing your own risk tolerance and matching it to your financial objectives is essential to making wise choices about where and how to invest.

There is a direct correlation between risk and reward; the more risk you are ready to accept, the greater the chance of both better profits and higher losses. Building a portfolio that fits your financial goals and your capacity for uncertainty tolerance requires an understanding of this equilibrium.

Investment risk can take many different forms. The whole market's general ups and downs are referred to as market risk. For instance, most equities often lose value during a recession. However, there is also company-specific risk, which is the possibility that a single company's performance may change as a result of management choices, new product introductions, or outside competition.

Risk exists even within particular industries; tech equities, for instance, are frequently far more volatile than utility stocks. Being aware of these dangers enables you to allocate your money more intelligently.

The prospective return on your investments, however, is known as reward. Investing with greater risk usually has the potential for greater returns. Investing in startups or emerging markets, for example, may be hazardous, but if the businesses or economies are successful, there may be significant profits.

Although they are less likely to provide rapid growth, more conservative investments, such government bonds or blue-chip stocks, typically offer more consistent returns. The secret is to decide how much danger you are ready to accept and how much profit you are looking for.

Your age, financial status, and investing objectives are just a few of the variables that will affect your individual risk tolerance. Younger investors may be more inclined to take on risk in the hopes of earning larger returns because they have a longer time horizon before retirement.

They can afford to ride out volatility and have more time to recover from market downturns. On the other hand, because they have less time to recoup from any losses, older investors or those who are getting close to retirement frequently prefer lower risk.

When it comes to risk management, it's also critical to take diversification into account. The impact of any one investment's bad performance can be lessened by distributing your money throughout other asset classes, such as stocks, bonds, and real estate. This reduces the overall risk to your portfolio since even if one investment underperforms, the others might help offset the losses.

The idea of "risk-adjusted returns" should be taken into account in addition to these other considerations. This entails evaluating the risk you're putting on in relation to the rewards you're getting. Although a large return could appear alluring, it might not be worth the danger if it comes with it. You can build a balanced portfolio that increases your chances of reaching your financial objectives while lowering needless risk by carefully assessing the risk-return profile of possible assets.

In the end, knowing how risk and reward are related will help you make wise investing choices. The secret to accumulating wealth is understanding your risk tolerance and choosing investments that complement your financial goals, whether you are investing for retirement savings, short-term income, or long-term growth.

Profit from Tax-Advantaged Accounts

Tax-advantaged accounts are effective instruments for quickening the accumulation of wealth. They enable people to either postpone or completely avoid paying taxes on their investment earnings. Strategic use of these accounts can help you develop your wealth more quickly than you would in a taxable investment account and drastically lower your tax burden.

Although there are many different kinds of tax-advantaged accounts, each with unique advantages, the most popular ones are Health Savings Accounts (HSAs), Traditional and Roth IRAs, and 401(k)s.

One of the most popular retirement accounts is a 401(k). Making pre-tax contributions to a 401(k) might reduce your current tax liability because they are subtracted from your annual taxable income. Your 401(k) assets grow tax-deferred, so you won't be taxed on capital gains, dividends, or interest until you take the money out, usually in retirement. Your investments can compound more effectively over time thanks to this tax deferral, which can eventually increase your retirement wealth.

In contrast, tax-free growth is provided by Roth IRAs. Although the money in a Roth IRA grows tax-free, contributions are made with after-tax cash, which means you do not receive a tax deduction at the time of contribution.

Additionally, if you fulfill certain requirements, you can take tax-free withdrawals in retirement. Because you won't have to pay taxes on the gains you've amassed over the years, Roth IRAs are especially alluring if you anticipate being in a higher tax rate when you retire.

There are yearly contribution caps on both of these accounts, so you may only make contributions up to a specific sum annually. You can increase your wealth considerably more quickly than you would in a taxable account, though, if you make the most of these limitations and contribute as much as you can. The tax advantages of Roth IRAs and 401(k)s can eventually cause a significant difference in the total amount of money you save for retirement.

Another kind of tax-advantaged account that is expressly intended for medical expenses is a Health Savings Account (HSA). But HSAs have a special benefit: they can also be utilized as a vehicle for retirement savings. Your taxable income is decreased when you make pre-tax contributions to an HSA. The money in the HSA also grows tax-free, and withdrawals for approved medical costs are tax-free as well. Although standard income taxes will apply, you can also take out HSA funds for non-medical purposes after the age of 65 without incurring penalties.

Contributing as much as you can and utilizing all of the tax advantages that tax-advantaged accounts offer are the keys to optimizing them. This could entail changing your monthly spending plan to put retirement savings first, especially if your company matches your 401(k) contributions. When compounded over time, even modest contributions can make a big difference in your long-term prosperity.

You can increase your wealth and reduce your tax obligations by utilizing tax-advantaged accounts. These accounts are crucial resources that can help you attain financial success more quickly, regardless of whether you're investing for retirement, medical costs, or other financial objectives.

Thought Room

How much risk do you feel comfortable taking on in your investments, and how does that affect the way you make financial decisions?

Do you currently utilize tax-advantaged accounts to their fullest potential? If not, what is preventing you from doing so?

What actions can you take right now to lower financial risk and improve portfolio diversification?

Chapter

5

Live Below Your Means

"Wealth is the ability to fully experience life." – Henry David Thoreau

Be Frugal Without Compromising Your Happiness.

Being frugal does not necessarily entail leading a life devoid of happiness or pleasure; rather, it involves making deliberate financial decisions to make sure that the items you do invest in and buy actually improve your quality of life. It's a frequent misperception that being frugal means sacrificing comfort and happiness in order to save money.

However, you can achieve both financial stability and personal fulfillment by being thrifty in a way that is consistent with your principles. Frugality, when practiced properly, can help you lead a happy life free from debt and needless financial strain.

Being aware is the secret to being thrifty without compromising your happiness. It's critical to assess what genuinely makes you happy and fulfilled. For example, cooking your own food instead of eating out a lot could make you feel more satisfied. Although eating out could make you feel happy for a short while, the long-term financial burden can make you less happy overall. As an alternative, you can save money and enjoy the satisfaction of making something yourself by spending time cooking at home. Frugality is a great weapon because it strikes a balance between conserving and savoring life's small joys.

Redefining what "luxury" means in your life is another requirement for adopting frugality. True luxury frequently resides in the caliber of relationships, experiences, and personal development, despite the fact that many people equate luxury with pricey brands or extravagant events. Spending time with family or taking a weekend trip to the outdoors, for instance, can be just as fulfilling as an expensive trip. You may make enduring memories without going over budget by selecting experiences that are consistent with your ideals.

Being selective about your financial investments will help you get rid of mental and physical clutter, which can increase your level of contentment.

It's also critical to understand that being thrifty does not entail giving up all pleasures. It's more about striking a balance. It's okay to occasionally enjoy a cup of coffee from your favorite café, but if frequenting them every day starts to cost you money, you might want to reevaluate whether that routine is actually making you happy.

Try substituting less expensive habits that nevertheless provide satisfaction for expensive ones rather than giving up all luxuries. You can make sure that every purchase or experience you have adds to a meaningful and satisfying life by being more deliberate about where and how you spend your money.

Additionally, being thrifty helps you change your perspective on money from one of being reactive to proactive. Because it allows you to base decisions on your long-term objectives rather than your whims, it promotes a sense of financial empowerment. You may get more control over your financial circumstances by creating a budget and conserving money, which can ultimately result in more peace of mind.

You can concentrate on what really important to you when you are not burdened by debt or pointless purchases. The key to leading a contented life without feeling the need to continuously spending is changing one's perspective.

In summary, being deliberate, aware, and disciplined with your spending is the key to being thrifty without compromising your enjoyment. It involves determining what genuinely makes you happy and giving those experiences top priority while keeping in mind how your financial decisions will affect your future. By adopting this strategy, you may build a life that is consistent with your goals and values in addition to securing a more secure financial future.

Put Your Financial Objectives Above Temporary Desires

A mentality change that puts future gains ahead of instant satisfaction is necessary to concentrate on long-term financial objectives. It can be difficult to resist the want to give in to the lure of rapid gratification in a world where quick purchases and fleeting pleasures are readily available. However, one of the most crucial steps to achieving long-term wealth and financial freedom is learning to put long-term financial stability ahead of immediate desires.

Knowing that every purchase you make now affects your future financial security is essential to striking this equilibrium. Indulging in something that captures your attention may make you feel good, but the pleasure is usually short-lived.

On the other hand, long-term financial freedom and peace of mind result from investing in your financial objectives, such as debt repayment, retirement savings, or emergency fund building. This calls for forethought, discipline, and a clear understanding of your objectives and their significance.

Making a thorough budget is a fantastic approach to practice setting financial goals in order of importance.

You can monitor where your money is going and spot areas where you could be splurging on items that don't help you achieve your long-term objectives by keeping track of your income and expenses.

Purchasing the newest technology or going out to eat many times a week, for instance, may not seem like much as first, but they can mount up over time and possibly take money away from more crucial savings objectives. Rather, you may make space for worthwhile investments that will position you for future success by readjusting your spending patterns to better reflect your objectives.

Dividing your bigger financial objectives into smaller, more achievable benchmarks will help you maintain discipline. If saving for retirement feels overwhelming, for instance, set a monthly savings target and then progressively raise your contributions over time.

Likewise, if debt repayment is a top priority, divide it into monthly goals and acknowledge minor accomplishments along the way. It will be simpler for you to stay on course and fight the temptation to spend money on things that won't improve your long-term financial situation if you concentrate on making small, steady gains.

The idea of "delayed gratification," which encourages people to postpone immediate rewards in favor of larger long-term gains, is another useful tactic. This can be delaying a luxury purchase to save for a home or skipping a trip now to increase your emergency fund. You can teach your mind to value waiting for greater rewards over giving in to the temptation of instant gratification by engaging in delayed gratification exercises. This way of thinking becomes engrained over time, which makes it simpler to maintain your financial objectives.

Surrounding yourself with others who share your financial objectives is also crucial. Having a support network, whether it be online communities, financial advisors, or accountability partners, can help you stick to your objectives. Speaking with people who have similar goals and understand your financial aspirations will encourage you to maintain your discipline and hold yourself accountable. As you strive for financial independence, discussing your success with others can also inspire you and give you a sense of achievement.

In the end, making short-term sacrifices to ensure long-term success is necessary on the path to financial security. You can make sure that your money is working for you rather than against you by setting financial objectives as a top priority and maintaining discipline in your spending patterns. Whether it's a debt-free life, a robust savings account, or a cozy retirement, the benefits of this methodical approach make the effort worthwhile.

Utilize Budgeting Tools to Monitor and Control Expenses

Technology provides us with strong tools to help us track and manage our finances in today's fast-paced environment. You may more effectively work toward your financial objectives and keep tabs on your spending patterns by using budgeting tools and applications. You can make better financial decisions, see where your money is going, and find places where you may make cuts to save more money by using these tools.

The capacity of budgeting software to automate the process of tracking spending is one of its main advantages. It might be simple to forget about little expenditures when using manual budgeting techniques, which makes it challenging to stick to your spending plan.

On the other hand, budgeting apps let you link your credit cards and bank accounts, giving you real-time spending information and automatically classifying your purchases. By saving you time and effort, this automation makes sure you don't overlook any financial information.

YNAB (You Need a Budget) and Mint, two well-known budgeting apps, provide comprehensive information about your financial situation and spending patterns. With the help of these applications, you can make personalized budgets according to your income and financial objectives, which makes it simpler to identify areas of overspending and make necessary adjustments.

To help you remain on track, they also offer you notifications and reminders. For example, they might remind you to pay your bills on time or notify you when you've gone over your budget in a certain area. Making educated judgments about where and how to spend your money can be greatly enhanced by the ease of having your financial data at your fingertips.

Setting and tracking financial goals is another benefit of using budgeting software. The majority of budgeting applications let you set clear objectives and monitor your progress over time, whether you're saving for an emergency fund, paying off credit card debt, or making plans for a big purchase. As you watch your financial objectives materialize, this function may be very satisfying as it keeps you motivated and gives you a visual depiction of your success.

Budgeting applications not only keep you on track and organized, but they also give you insightful information about your spending habits. To help you see where your money is going, many apps separate your costs into categories like grocery, entertainment, utilities, and more.

This breakdown might help you identify areas where you might be spending too much or where you could make changes to free up more money for debt repayment or savings. For example, you can make a goal to cut back on eating out if you find that you're spending too much on it. The money you save can then be used for something more significant, like emergency savings.

Finally, financial reporting and analysis functions that help you better comprehend your entire financial condition are frequently included in budgeting software. These programs can produce reports that give you a thorough understanding of your financial situation by displaying your spending patterns, income compared to expenses, and net worth. You can use this research to find long-term trends that may not be immediately apparent and adapt as needed to make sure you're reaching your financial objectives.

To sum up, budgeting apps and tools are a great way to take charge of your money and make sure you're moving closer to your financial objectives. You can attain financial security and freedom by automating the tracking of your expenditures, establishing clear objectives, and examining your financial patterns.

Thought Room

Which aspects of your life do you spend money on that don't support your long-term objectives?

How can you resist the want to give short-term pleasures priority over long-term wealth accumulation?

Which budgeting tool or technique has proven most effective for you, and why?

Chapter 6

Diversify Your Income Streams for Wealth Growth

"Don't put all your eggs in one basket." – Warren Buffett

Establish Passive Income Streams.

Creating methods that enable money to flow into your account without your regular involvement is the key to building wealth, which goes beyond only earning money through active job. Passive income streams are extremely beneficial in this situation. Money produced with little to no effort following an initial time, money, or both investment is known as passive income.

While passive income enables you to make money while you sleep, travel, or concentrate on other activities, active income necessitates ongoing labor, such as a job or freelance employment. One of the best strategies to accumulate long-term wealth in the modern world, where achieving financial independence is a widespread goal, is to establish passive income streams.

Online companies including blogging, e-book creation, and online course launches are among the most well-liked ways to get passive income. These platforms take a lot of time and work up front, but once they are up and running, they may be quite lucrative.

With minimal effort beyond marketing and customer support, you can sell the product for as long as you want after it is created. In a similar vein, affiliate marketing provides a means of making money by endorsing the goods of others. Recurring commissions can be earned by promoting goods and services once you have a following or platform.

Purchasing rental properties is another excellent way to generate passive income. Rental properties provide steady income flow through monthly rent payments, and real estate has traditionally been seen as a means of achieving financial success.

Although purchasing real estate necessitates a substantial initial outlay of funds, the return on that investment can be substantial. The property may increase in value over time in addition to generating rental revenue, providing for both short-term and long-term advantages.

Real estate investment trusts (REITs) offer an alternative for people who are not prepared to assume the management of real estate. REITs provide a passive approach to generate income from real estate without actually owning a property by pooling the funds of several investors to purchase and manage properties.

Purchasing dividend-paying stocks is another way to generate passive income in the digital age. You can get a consistent income without having to sell your shares if you buy stock in companies that pay dividends on a regular basis. These dividends can be reinvested for compound growth and are normally handed out on a quarterly basis.

With many well-known corporations paying consistent dividends, dividend stocks have the advantage of being generally stable. Even if you're not actively managing your assets, you can generate a steady income stream over time by picking stocks well and holding them for a long period.

Peer-to-peer lending services can give you the chance to lend money to people or businesses and generate passive income. By serving as middlemen, these platforms enable investors to make direct loans to borrowers in return for interest payments. The gains can be significant, but the risk may be greater than with conventional investments.

Peer-to-peer lending can be an interesting and lucrative way to generate passive income for investors who are ready to diversify their holdings, but it's crucial to carefully consider risk.

Lastly, recurring revenue streams can be generated via intellectual property rights, such as royalties from music, books, patents, or photographs. Once intellectual property has been created, it can continue to make money for a long time. Royalties are frequently a source of passive income for musicians, authors, and inventors. If you are talented enough to produce something unique, you can make money passively while also helping others by licensing your work.

In conclusion, diversified sources of income is essential to accumulating long-term wealth. Although it isn't a quick fix, passive income can offer long-term financial stability if it is developed carefully. You can increase your wealth accumulation and supplement your active income by spending time and money on systems that provide revenue with little effort. As they say, "Make money work for you, not the other way around."

Invest in Real Estate to Build Wealth Over Time

For generations, real estate has been a tried-and-true strategy for accumulating wealth, and it is still one of the most effective ways to create lasting wealth. The possibility for both capital growth and income production is what makes real estate so alluring. Whether you're investing in commercial real estate, flipping homes, or renting out buildings, real estate offers a special set of benefits that other investment vehicles might not match.

The steady cash flow that real estate investing offers through rental revenue is its primary advantage. Rent payments from tenants can create a consistent revenue stream for you when you buy a rental property, whether it be residential or commercial. Investing in real estate in high-demand locations might make this a dependable source of income.

Your mortgage and maintenance expenses can be paid for using rental income, and whatever money left over turns into a profit. The property gets even more profitable as you pay down the mortgage over time. Furthermore, rental income can increase in line with inflation with a carefully selected investment, guaranteeing that your profits will grow over time.

Real estate delivers substantial capital appreciation in addition to cash flow. Properties typically appreciate in value over time, especially in places that are seeing urbanization or population growth. For instance, if property values increase, purchasing a home in a gentrifying district or close to major infrastructural developments might result in significant profits.

Taking advantage of these tendencies in appreciation, many investors buy real estate with the goal of selling it for more money. Often called "flipping," this tactic can yield significant gains, particularly in a favorable market.

Additionally, real estate investing gives investors some degree of control over their money. In contrast to stocks, which are influenced by the market and subject to unpredictable fluctuations, real estate gives you the ability to make choices that have a direct impact on the value of the property.

Real estate offers you more alternatives to raise the property's value, whether it is through remodeling, curb appeal improvement, or functional enhancement. You can generate opportunities for both immediate and long-term financial advantage by managing properties.

The possibility of tax advantages is an additional benefit of real estate investing. Tax deductions for mortgage interest, property taxes, maintenance costs, and depreciation are frequently available to property owners. Property owners can significantly lower their taxable income by using depreciation to write off the expense of the property's worth over time. Your net profits can be greatly increased by these tax advantages, which also improve the appeal of real estate investing.

Investing in real estate can also act as a hedge against inflation. The cost of living, including rent and property values, increases in tandem with inflation. This means that real estate may keep up with inflation and, in many cases, outperform it, in contrast to investments in typical accounts that may lose value over time.

Real estate has an advantage since it is a physical asset, particularly during uncertain economic times. When inflation puts pressure on other areas of the economy, real estate values typically maintain their value or even rise.

Another flexible investing choice is real estate. There are many different kinds of real estate investments to fit different tastes and objectives, whether you're interested in single-family homes, multi-family apartments, vacation rentals, or commercial buildings. You can lower risk and raise the possibility of consistent returns by diversifying your real estate holdings.

To sum up, there are several ways to build money through real estate investing. Real estate is still one of the greatest long-term investment options because of its steady income flow, appreciation potential, tax benefits, and inflation hedging. There is always a chance to create long-term wealth through real estate investing, regardless of your level of experience.

Purchasing Dividend Stocks and Other Assets That Produce Income

Income-producing assets, such as dividend stocks, have a special chance to gradually increase wealth.

Dividend stocks give investors regular payouts, usually on a quarterly basis, in contrast to growth stocks, which concentrate on price appreciation.

They are a desirable choice for anyone wishing to generate a passive income stream and augment their active income due to their consistent income stream. Since reinvested dividends can greatly increase long-term profits, the appeal of dividend investing is not just in the income but also in the power of compounding.

Stocks that generate dividends provide a steady flow of income that can help you reach your financial objectives or pay for living needs without having to liquidate your investment. Many well-known businesses have a track record of consistently paying dividends, particularly in industries like consumer products, energy, and healthcare.

These businesses are secure investments for long-term revenue because they often have steady cash flow and sound business plans. Dividend payments can add up to a sizable sum over time, particularly if they are reinvested to buy further shares, which will enable you to take advantage of both the income and the compounding impact.

The capacity of dividend equities to serve as a buffer during market downturns is one of their primary benefits. Although market volatility may cause stock values to fluctuate, dividends give a steady return and some degree of stability even in unpredictable markets.

Strong financial firms may continue to pay dividends during recessions or bear markets, giving investors income even if the value of their portfolios drops. Because of this, dividend stocks are a desirable choice for investors who are risk averse and seek consistent profits without having to keep a close eye on the market.

In addition to the income they offer, dividend stocks also have the potential to increase in value. The stock prices of many companies that pay dividends also rise steadily, particularly those in dependable industries with a track record of success. Long-term holders of these companies may benefit from both dividend income and capital growth, providing them with the best of both worlds. Dividend stocks are a well-rounded option for accumulating wealth because of their consistent payouts and potential for stock price rise.

Your efforts to accumulate wealth can be further strengthened by other income-producing assets in addition to dividend stocks. High-yield savings accounts, real estate crowdfunding, and peer-to-peer lending all provide chances for consistent profits without the need for active management.

You can lend money directly to people or businesses using peer-to-peer lending services and receive interest on your investment. Similar to this, real estate crowdfunding enables you to combine your funds with those of other investors to finance real estate projects, with the potential to profit from appreciation and rental revenue. Despite being more cautious, high-yield savings accounts offer interest on your investments with little risk.

To sum up, investing in dividend stocks and other assets that generate income is a tried-and-true strategy for gradually increasing wealth. You can build a solid financial foundation that enables you to concentrate on long-term objectives by concentrating on assets that generate consistent income.

These investments offer the consistent cash flow required to promote financial independence and augment active income, whether in the form of dividends, interest, or rental income.

Thought Room

What actions can you take right now to lessen your dependency on a single source of income and begin diversifying it?

Are you prepared to make the move, and how can real estate investments fit into your long-term wealth-building plan?

What kinds of assets could you look into to increase your passive income?

Chapter 7

Master Debt Management for Wealth Preservation

"It's not about how much money you make. It's about how much you keep." – Robert Kiyosaki

Get Rid of High-Interest Debt Fast

High-interest debt is one of the biggest obstacles that many people encounter while trying to develop money. Payday loans, credit card debt, personal loans, and other high-interest borrowing can rapidly undermine your financial security, making it more difficult to invest or save. Your potential to build wealth is hampered by the higher interest rates you pay the longer you keep high-interest debt. Addressing this debt directly is one of the first and most important stages in creating wealth.

One barrier that exacerbates your financial problems is high-interest debt. For instance, the interest rate on a regular credit card debt may be 20% or more, which can quickly raise your debt balance. Consider having a $5,000 balance on a credit card that has a 20% interest rate.

You might have to spend thousands more in interest and take years to pay it off if you only make the minimal payments. This puts people in a debt cycle by limiting their ability to invest or increase their wealth. It takes a clear approach to break free.

An approach that is frequently used to address high-interest debt is the debt avalanche method. This approach recommends paying the minimum amount due on other bills and giving priority to the ones with the highest interest rates. You can reduce the amount of interest paid over time and hasten the process of becoming debt-free by paying off the most expensive obligations first.

If you have many credit cards with different interest rates, for example, you will save the most money if you concentrate on paying off the card with the highest interest rate. You can proceed to the next obligation with the highest interest rate after paying off the one with the highest interest rate, and so on.

An additional well-liked tactic is the debt snowball method. This approach suggests paying off the smallest debt first, regardless of interest rate, in order to build momentum rather than concentrating on the interest rate. This method gives psychological advantages even though it might not save as much on interest. You get immediate benefits from paying off smaller loans, which encourages you to keep taking on bigger debts. This technique can be especially useful for people who require a mental boost to maintain motivation, transforming the process of paying off debt into a string of small successes.

The secret to getting rid of high-interest debt is dedication and self-control, regardless of the approach taken. To increase the amount of money you have available for debt repayment, review your monthly budget and find areas where you may cut back on discretionary spending.

Reducing unnecessary spending on things like eating out, subscription services, and impulsive purchases might help free up funds so that debt repayment can take precedence. You may put money toward investments and savings sooner if you pay off high-interest debt as soon as possible.

Consolidating high-interest debts into one lower-interest loan could also be beneficial. Several high-interest debts are combined into a single loan through debt consolidation, frequently with a lower interest rate. This enables you to concentrate on a single loan instead of managing several payments. Consolidation loans with fees or unfavorable terms should be avoided, nevertheless. Make sure consolidation makes long-term financial sense by analyzing your options before deciding to go with it.

Although getting rid of high-interest debt can be difficult, it's an essential first step on the path to financial independence. You will have the financial space you need to concentrate on accumulating wealth if you act quickly, using tried-and-true debt-reduction techniques, and maintain discipline in your approach.

Build Wealth Using Smart Debt

Although debt is frequently seen negatively, not all debt is harmful. In actuality, some forms of debt can be effective instruments for accumulating wealth. Understanding the difference between "good debt" and "bad debt" and how to use each effectively are crucial. Generally speaking, good debt is employed for assets that will increase in value or yield income over time. Conversely, bad debt—such as credit card debt or personal loans for non-essential purchases—is utilized for consumption.

A mortgage is an excellent example of positive debt. Even though mortgages need interest payments, the value of the property you buy with the loan may rise over time. With a mortgage, you can use the bank's funds to purchase an asset that may increase in value rather than using up all of your assets to buy a house entirely. Since real estate usually increases in value over time, the money you borrow now to buy a property could greatly boost your net worth later on.

In a similar vein, student loans may also qualify as good debt if they are taken out to fund an education that increases one's earning potential. Student loans are a wise investment in your future since higher education can greatly boost your earning potential.

Making sure your chosen course of study offers a clear route to better-paying work is crucial. Over the course of a career, a degree in a highly sought-after industry, like technology, engineering, or healthcare, for instance, can generate substantial returns, making the initial loan outlay justifiable.

Business loans are another type of useful debt. Borrowing money to invest in your business can be a terrific strategy to develop wealth if you have a good business idea or an established business with room to grow.

You can expand your business, hire more staff, or buy equipment that will increase efficiency with the help of business loans. When properly executed, this kind of borrowing can boost sales for your company and generate wealth through expansion in ownership and equity.

It takes discipline and careful preparation to use good debt strategically. It's crucial to make sure that any loan is utilized to build wealth or boost future earnings. Wealth can be created, for example, by taking out a loan to buy assets like real estate or by investing in education that will lead to a higher-paying career.

Financial difficulties can arise, though, if debt is taken on for unproductive reasons, such as funding a lifestyle or purchasing deteriorating goods. Always exercise caution when considering the debt's intended use and make sure it complements your long-term financial objectives.

Effectively managing good debt is also crucial. Pay your bills on time, monitor your interest rates, and refrain from taking on more debt than you can handle. You can expand your assets and financial stability by deliberately employing excellent debt to leverage other people's money and gradually accumulate wealth.

Increase Your Credit to Take Advantage of Better Financial Opportunities

One of the most effective financial instruments you may have is a high credit score. Your capacity to borrow money at advantageous rates is determined by your credit score, and a high score can lead to a number of financial options, such as credit cards, business loans, auto loans, and mortgages.

Over time, a higher credit score can result in reduced interest rates, which can save you a substantial sum of money. For instance, over the course of a loan, a borrower with a high credit score might spend hundreds or even thousands of dollars less in interest than a borrower with a low score.

Knowing what influences a credit score is the first step to achieving a high one. Payment history, credit utilization, duration of credit history, categories of credit used, and current inquiries are the five main components that go into calculating credit scores.

Your payment history, which makes up 35% of your credit score, is the most significant component. It's critical to pay off all of your debts on schedule because defaults, bankruptcies, and late payments can lower your credit score.

Then, as it makes up 30% of your score, concentrate on keeping your credit utilization ratio low. Your overall credit card balances divided by your total credit limits yields this ratio. It is advised that you keep your credit use below 30% in order to preserve a high credit score. This demonstrates to lenders that you manage your borrowing responsibly and don't rely too much on credit. To prevent carrying large credit card amounts, try to pay them off in full each month.

The duration of your credit history, which makes about 15% of your score, is another crucial component. Your credit score will benefit more the longer you have credit accounts in good standing. Old accounts should not be closed because they increase your credit history and raise your score. Additionally, vary your credit mix to demonstrate to lenders that you are capable of handling a variety of credit forms, including revolving credit (like credit cards) and installment loans (like mortgages or student loans).

Finally, reduce how many hard inquiries appear on your credit report. Your credit score may be somewhat lowered when the lender conducts a rigorous inquiry when you apply for new credit. Hard inquiries are a common component of the loan application process, but if you receive too many in a short amount of time, it may be a sign of financial trouble and lower your credit score. Pay attention to how many credit applications you file, particularly if you intend to buy a big item quickly, like a house or a car.

Securing advantageous financial prospects requires establishing and preserving a high credit score. You may build a solid credit profile that leads to better loans, cheaper interest rates, and more financial stability by continuously managing your debt, paying your bills on time, and maintaining a low credit utilization rate.

Thought Room

How do you plan to pay off high-interest debt, and what are some ways to speed up the process?

How can you strategically exploit whatever "good debt" you may have that you could use to increase your wealth?

What steps can you do right now to raise your credit score and how does it influence your financial decisions?

Conclusion

Well done on finishing this journey through the techniques and knowledge that will enable you to take charge of your money and create a safe, wealthy future. You've just discovered useful strategies, techniques, and attitudes that will enable you to become financially independent before you are forty. By reading and considering these ideas, you are making an investment in your future self that will pay out in the years to come.

You will have more control over the course of your life the earlier you start managing your money. Being financially stable as you approach middle age is not a luxury; it is a need. It enables you to make empowered decisions, achieve financial independence, and follow your hobbies.

Keep in mind that achieving financial success before the age of forty is about more than just money; it's about giving yourself choices, peace of mind, and the flexibility to live your life as you see fit. There is a limited window of opportunity to acquire wealth, particularly in your 30s. You can change the way you live in your 40s and beyond by making the correct choices today.

Let's review the main points you learnt from each chapter and their significance for your financial future.

You learned about the potential of generating many revenue sources, especially passive ones, in the first chapter, "Create Passive Income Streams to Supplement Active Income." This is important in midlife because depending only on your active income can leave you exposed to life's unforeseen turns.

You can devote more time and effort to increasing your wealth by generating passive income through investments, side ventures, or royalties. This paves the way for financial freedom and enables you to work smarter, not harder.

Proceeding to the following phase, you discovered how real estate may serve as a fundamental component of your wealth-building plan in "Invest in Real Estate for Long-Term Wealth." Real estate has a tendency to increase in value over time and can offer a steady source of income, in contrast to the erratic nature of stocks or commercial endeavors. Investing in real estate with growth potential ensures your financial legacy by building long-term wealth that can be inherited by future generations.

You learned how dividend stocks, bonds, and other income-producing assets can provide a consistent income stream while also increasing in value over time in "The Benefits of Investing in Dividend Stocks and Other Income-Generating Assets."

These investments provide you with the financial stability you need to weather any storm in addition to enabling you to make money while you sleep. One of the best financial decisions you can make is to learn how to use your money to generate more income through interest and dividends.

The impact that high-interest debt, such as credit card bills, might have on your financial future was then discussed in "Eliminate High-Interest Debt Quickly." You now know that you can quickly pay off this debt by employing strategies like the debt avalanche or snowball strategy, which will free up more money for investments and savings. Instead of paying interest to other people, a debt-free lifestyle enables you to reinvest your money where it counts most—increasing wealth.

You were reminded in "Use Good Debt to Build Wealth" that not all debt is bad. In actuality, some debt—such as school loans or mortgages—can be used as leverage to increase wealth over the long run. Your capacity to grow your assets and expand your financial possibilities can be greatly improved by knowing how to strategically employ good debt rather than completely shun it.

You acknowledged in "Build Your Credit to Improve Financial Opportunities" how crucial it is to keep your credit score high. Better loan conditions, reduced interest rates, and more advantageous financial prospects are all made possible by having a high credit score. Your credit is an essential weapon in your wealth-building toolbox, whether you're trying to start a business, buy a home, or make other significant investments.

Let's now take a moment to consider the implications of all of this for your financial future. These chapters have taught you more than simply theoretical knowledge. These are doable actions you can start taking right now to make sure you're headed in the correct direction before you turn forty. Time, however, is of the essential.

The earlier you begin, the easier it is to compound your efforts and the more momentum you might get. It's more important to make consistent progress toward your financial objectives than to accomplish everything at once.

Now that you have the blueprint, it is time to act. Now is the perfect moment to put everything you've learnt into practice if you've reached this stage and are feeling inspired. Determine how much debt you currently have by first evaluating your financial status. Are you making long-term investments? What chances do you have for passive income? Whether it's settling a high-interest loan, opening a brokerage account, or researching possible real estate opportunities, start today.

The most important lesson here is that you must have a strong financial base prior to reaching midlife. Situations change as we age, and the financial choices you make in your twenties and thirties will influence your forties and beyond.

Although it's not too late to start, you'll have more clout later on if you take the initiative now. Your ability to assist loved ones, pursue your aspirations, and retire comfortably may be limited if you don't begin growing your fortune before the age of forty.

As you proceed, keep in mind that achieving financial success takes time and is not random. Discipline, consistency, and well-informed decision-making are the foundations of it. By reading this book and deciding to alter your life, you've already taken a significant step. Deliberate action is the next stage. Make tiny, doable adjustments at first, then expand from there.

In summary, the foundation of financial success is the removal of high-interest debt, the strategic use of good debt, credit building, real estate investing, the creation of passive income streams, and wise investment choices. You'll be giving yourself the best chance to live a financially free life and position yourself for long-term success if you start now, before you turn 40.

I implore you to take action now. Your future self will be appreciative. You can achieve the financial independence and tranquility you seek, but only if you take charge of your financial future right away. Make these adjustments now rather than later.

YOU CAN MAKE WEALTH BEFORE 40!

www.ingramcontent.com/pod-product-compliance
Lightning Source LLC
Chambersburg PA
CBHW050309230526
45471CB00005B/2091